599.532
HER   Herriges, Ann

           Dolphins

DATE DUE

MY 18 '02	SE 1 9 '74		
	MY - 5 '75		
NO 2 '02	EF 1 8 '76		
	7 3 '7		
MR - 3 '09	AP 13		
SE 9 '09			
SE 2 3 '09			
JA 2 5 '12	MR 7 7 '78		
MR 1 2 '12			
1 5			

OCEANS ALIVE

Dolphins

by Ann Herriges

BELLWETHER MEDIA • MINNEAPOLIS, MN

BLASTOFF!
2
READERS

Note to Librarians, Teachers, and Parents:

Blastoff! Readers are carefully developed by literacy experts and combine standards-based content with developmentally appropriate text.

Level 1 provides the most support through repetition of high-frequency words, light text, predictable sentence patterns, and strong visual support.

Level 2 offers early readers a bit more challenge through varied simple sentences, increased text load, and less repetition of high-frequency words.

Level 3 advances early-fluent readers toward fluency through increased text and concept load, less reliance on visuals, longer sentences, and more literary language.

Whichever book is right for your reader, Blastoff! Readers are the perfect books to build confidence and encourage a love of reading that will last a lifetime!

This edition first published in 2007 by Bellwether Media.

No part of this publication may be reproduced in whole or in part without written permission of the publisher. For information regarding permission, write to Bellwether Media Inc., Attention: Permissions Department, Post Office Box 1C, Minnetonka, MN 55345-9998.

Library of Congress Cataloging-in-Publication Data
Herriges, Ann.
  Dolphins / by Ann Herriges.
    p. cm. — (Blastoff! readers) (Oceans alive!)
Summary: "Simple text and supportive images introduce beginning readers to dolphins. Intended for students in kindergarten through third grade."
  Includes bibliographical references and index.
  ISBN-10: 1-60014-017-3 (hardcover : alk. paper)
  ISBN-13: 978-1-60014-017-4 (hardcover : alk. paper)
  1. Dolphins—Juvenile literature. I. Title. II. Series. III. Series: Oceans alive!

  QL737.C432H458 2007
  599.53—dc22   2006005360

Table of Contents

Splash! Dolphins jump above the ocean waves.

4

Dolphins are **mammals**.

Some dolphins are as small as a person.

Some dolphins are bigger than a bus. **Orcas** are the biggest dolphins.

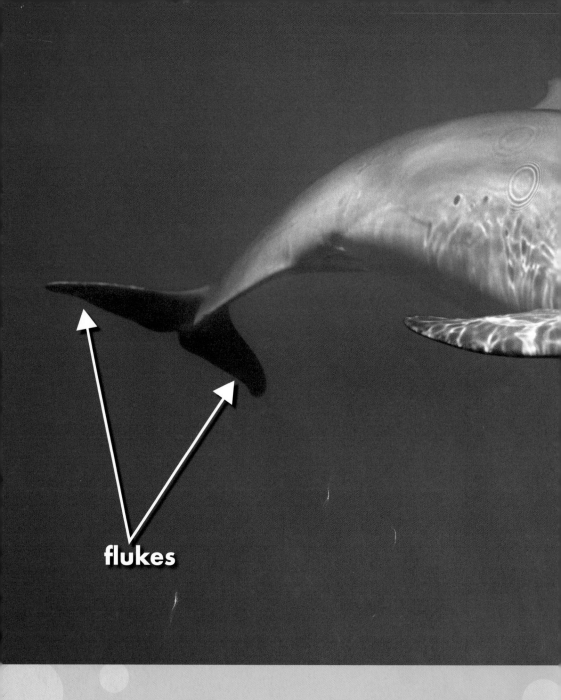

flukes

A dolphin tail has two fins
called **flukes**.

Dolphins move their tails up and down to swim.

9

Dolphins have two **flippers**. They use their flippers to turn and to stop.

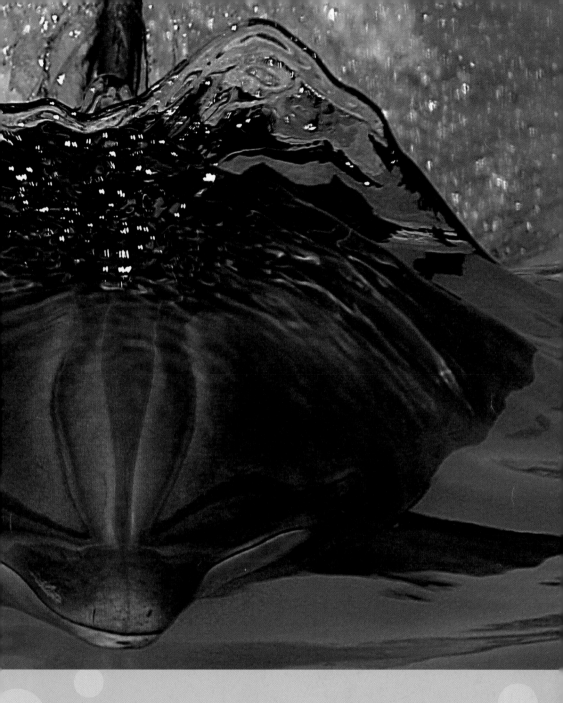

Dolphins have smooth skin.
It helps them slide through
the water.

11

dorsal fin

Dolphins have a **dorsal fin**. It keeps them from rolling over when they swim.

blowhole

Dolphins breathe air through a **blowhole**.

Dolphins have more than
100 sharp teeth.

14

They use their teeth to
catch fish and other food.

Dolphins hunt for food in groups called **pods**.

Dolphins make clicking sounds to find food. The sounds bounce off fish and make **echoes**.

Dolphins listen to the echoes.
The echoes tell dolphins
where the fish are.

Dolphins make sounds to talk to each other. They bark, chirp, and whistle.

19

Dolphins like to play. They flip and twist together in the air.

Dolphins are friendly. They even have smiles on their faces!

Glossary

blowhole—a breathing hole at the top of an ocean mammal's head; dolphins use muscles to close the blowhole when they are underwater.

dorsal fin—the fin on the back of an ocean animal

echo—a sound that repeats over and over after it bounces off an object

flipper—a wide, flat limb that some ocean animals use to swim

flukes—the two fins at the end of a dolphin's tail

mammal—an animal with a backbone that is warm-blooded and has hair; mammals are born alive and drink their mother's milk.

orcas—large black-and-white ocean mammals; orcas are the the largest dolphins.

pod—a group of ocean mammals

To Learn More

AT THE LIBRARY

Andreae, Giles. *Commotion in the Ocean.* Wilton, Conn.: Tiger Tales, 2002.

Berger, Melvin and Gilda. *Splash! A Book about Whales and Dolphins.* New York: Scholastic, 2001.

Davis, Lambert. *Swimming with Dolphins.* New York: Blue Sky Press, 2004.

Marciano, John Bemelmans. *There's a Dolphin in the Grand Canal.* New York: Viking, 2005.

Pfeffer, Wendy. *Dolphin Talk: Whistles, Clicks, and Clapping Jaws.* New York: HarperCollins, 2003.

Wallace, Karen. *Diving Dolphin.* New York: Dorling Kindersley, 2001.

ON THE WEB

Learning more about dolphins is as easy as 1, 2, 3.

1. Go to www.factsurfer.com

2. Enter "dolphins" into search box.

3. Click the "Surf" button and you will see a list of related web sites.

With factsurfer.com, finding more information is just a click away.

Index

The photographs in this book are reproduced through the courtesy of : Jeffrey L. Rotman/Getty Images, front cover; SBI/NASA/Getty Images, p. 4; Frank Greenaway/Getty Images, p. 5, Michael Melford/Getty Images, pp. 6-7; Mike Hill/Alamy, pp. 8-9; blickwinkel/Alamy, pp. 10-11; Theo Allofs/Getty Images, pp. 12-13; Jeff Schiller, p. 14; Jeff Hunter/Getty Images, p. 15; Stephen Frink Collection/Alamy, pp. 16-17, 18-19, Gail Shumway/Getty Images, p. 20, Lloyd Luecke, p. 21.